Mastering Your Emotions

Steps to Reject the Spirit of Fear

Shawnee Neal

Sunshine & Faith Publishing, LLC

Mastering Your Emotions: Steps to Reject the Spirit of Fear

Copyright © 2025 by Shawnee Neal

ISBN: 978-1-7355688-8-1

Sunshine & Faith Publishing

www.sunshineandfaithpublishing.com

Unless expressly stated, all scripture references taken from the Holy Bible, New International Version®, NIV® Copyright ©1973, 1978, 1984, 2011 by Biblica, Inc.®: Used by permission. All rights reserved worldwide.

All rights reserved. The publisher's prior written permission is required before anyone reproduces, stores in a retrieval system, or transmits any part of this publication in any form or by any means, including electronic, digital, mechanical, photocopying, or recording.

Disclaimer

The author cannot provide diagnostic or therapeutic services via social media as a mental health professional. You should not use this book to treat mental health concerns; it is for educational purposes only. You should consult your primary healthcare provider or counselor for medical or mental health advice. The author assumes no responsibility whatsoever under any circumstances for any actions taken as a result of the information contained.

Contents

Dedication		V
Preface		VI
1.	How Does Fear Affect You?	1
2.	Knowing Your Authority in Christ	10
3.	Understanding God's Promises	17
4.	Humble Prayer	25
5.	Meditate on Scripture	31
6.	An Act of Faith	38
7.	Support from Your Community	45
8.	Worship and Praise	51
9.	Healing from the Root of Fear	57
10.	The Power of Walking in Faith	64
11.	About the Author	69

Dedication

To my husband, Adriel. Thank you for supporting me!

Preface

Emotions are a powerful expression of how we experience life. Emotions can be beautiful and ugly. No matter the emotion, there's always a story behind it. I've experienced many emotions throughout my life, but the most challenging one is fear. When I look back at my life, fear always found its way into different areas. The earliest memory that I can recall is of living in a household where arguing often took place. I remember spending a lot of time in my bedroom to avoid hearing it. The loud voices, absurd words, and the adults' physical postures in my life caused great fear and concern for the well-being of everyone in the house. I often woke up and heard random arguments during the midnight hours. These encounters occurred so frequently that they became the norm. Although I had gotten used to it, my nervous system could never regulate itself. It seemed the more I heard arguing, the more fearful I became. I believe it shifted something inside me, causing me to produce fearful thoughts about myself and the world at a young age. As I look back at those times, I realize that fear provoked in a child can cause a lifetime of pain.

Dedication

To my husband, Adriel. Thank you for supporting me!

Preface

Emotions are a powerful expression of how we experience life. Emotions can be beautiful and ugly. No matter the emotion, there's always a story behind it. I've experienced many emotions throughout my life, but the most challenging one is fear. When I look back at my life, fear always found its way into different areas. The earliest memory that I can recall is of living in a household where arguing often took place. I remember spending a lot of time in my bedroom to avoid hearing it. The loud voices, absurd words, and the adults' physical postures in my life caused great fear and concern for the well-being of everyone in the house. I often woke up and heard random arguments during the midnight hours. These encounters occurred so frequently that they became the norm. Although I had gotten used to it, my nervous system could never regulate itself. It seemed the more I heard arguing, the more fearful I became. I believe it shifted something inside me, causing me to produce fearful thoughts about myself and the world at a young age. As I look back at those times, I realize that fear provoked in a child can cause a lifetime of pain.

Even as an adult, I am in a state of recovery from what fear tried to do to me. I know it wanted to silence me, stop me from pursuing my dreams, and make me believe I was unworthy of happiness frequently. Today, I am grateful to stand on my two feet, claiming victory over fear!

Throughout this book, I will share more of my testimony and how God set me free from the troubles that fear brought me. I used to feel like a slave to it, and you may be in the same position. You may feel rejected and used up by fear, but I'm here to tell you to hold on a little longer. In a short while, you will lose fear and gain peace. I want you to have high expectations for what God has in store. Remember, I am just a vessel sharing my story to bring you closer to the promises that God has already given you. It is no secret that the enemy comes to steal, kill, and destroy. When you look at fear, you can define it by the effect that it has on you. It can cause you to miss out on experiences, your destiny, and your hopes and dreams. That's a lot of damage.

I recall the first encounter with fear. It was in the fifth grade. I was casually walking up to the school to start my day when I overheard a boy calling my name. I looked to my left and noticed it was the cute, popular boy at school, standing next to two of his guy friends. I instantly put my head down and walked right past them. When I look back on that day, I recall the intense fear that I had. My body froze up, and I felt heat rush from the bottom of my spine to the top of my head. I also had heavy breathing and couldn't stop replaying the scenario as I kept walking away. I later got to my class and daydreamed about it all day, and then it was a thought that I couldn't shake. I would tell myself, "Why won't you just say hello back? Why are you not speaking back?" I was upset with myself for responding the way I did. But I was never the type to be sociable and kept quiet in school most of the time. I had this burning desire not to shut down while around people, but I didn't know how to stop it. I'm sure this incident isn't the first time fear has affected me, but it is the one I will never forget. It was the first time that I had tried to fight back the fear through self-talk and motivational statements. This incident only happened because the same incident with the boy occurred 2-3 other times; it was the last time I had talked back. I secretly had a crush on this boy, but I told no one, so it was surprising when he liked me. Well, I presumed he liked me because he and his friends were nice to me and started conversations, even though I ignored them every time. They never got angry or seemed upset, so one day I convinced myself I would be confident and friendly, saying hello and smiling.

After I built up the courage and felt 110% that I would respond, I stopped seeing the guy with his friends, and from that day forward, he stopped making attempts and giving me eye contact. That was a pivotal moment in my life, where I learned that if I didn't speak up, I'd miss out on an opportunity. Well, this wasn't a serious opportunity in reality, but as a fifth grader, it was a pretty big deal for me. But the thoughts engraved in me pushed me to fight and conquer. I knew that I'd have to make a choice: either fear would get the best of me, or I'd get the best of fear. At that age, I knew of God, but I did not know it was Him speaking to me, not my strength. I soon realized that I could hear Him and knew that I could talk to Him at any time. While I didn't understand the magnitude of relying on God, I knew it was my only haven, because who else felt safe enough to share these challenges with? I didn't have a safe person to talk to, and, to be honest, I'm glad God taught me at a young age to rely on Him, not others. Later in life, this made it easier for me not to idolize people, but it didn't stop me from making poor decisions about people.

As you read this book, you will have a scripture at the end of each chapter to meditate on. God instructs us in Joshua 1:8, "Keep this

Book of the Law always on your lips; meditate on it day and night, so that you may be careful to do everything written in it. Then you will be prosperous and successful." The power of meditating on God's word is that you come more into alignment with His word, which brings you into the promises of God. Also, the scripture states that you will be prosperous and successful. God's natural design is for his children to live in peace and succeed, so we have his commandments and word to instruct us on how to live in this world. We know that fear does the opposite: it causes you to adopt a poverty mindset and produce poor outcomes in life.

You can meditate by reciting the scripture as many times as possible, using it as a journal prompt to write your thoughts, or formulating it into an affirmation to post on your mirror.

Meditating on God's word produces:

- Improved memory recall, allowing you to pray the word of God with ease.

- Deeper reflection on the word and its meaning.

- Increased faith and peace in challenging areas of life.

Besides the scriptures, there will be some biblical affirmations. I've provided the affirmations to help you agree with God's word and apply it to your daily life. This book mainly quotes scripture because that is the proper strategy for rejecting the spirit of fear. Fear has been talking to you your whole life; it's time for you to take control of your thoughts and dismantle the words, sounds, and behaviors attached to them. This book will help you get on the right track to creating a healthier mindset and habits. So grab a pen, notebook, or an electronic device to take notes on, and let's get started!

Scripture Meditation: 1 John 4:18 (KJV) There is no fear in love; but perfect love casteth out fear: because fear hath torment. He that feareth is not made perfect in love.

Biblical Affirmation: I am a child of God, and he supplies me with everything I need!

How Does Fear Affect You?

Thoughts and feelings of fear can derive from many avenues. The relationship I built with fear throughout my life made it hard for me to detach from it. I used to wake up with fear and go to sleep, enabling it. I started building a relationship with fear at the early age of 5, after losing my grandmother. While I didn't fully understand death, I can recall the feeling of emptiness I felt seeing my maternal grandmother in the casket at her funeral. It was such a vivid moment that it is still a heavy image in my mind as an adult. Standing at the casket, I recall feeling alone, hurting that she was gone forever. I do not remember whether I cried, but as an adult, I can see my five-year-old body sitting on the pew at the funeral home, feeling detached from the room. I needed consoling but didn't know how to seek it. Everyone around me seemed sad, but no one could see my sadness. Someone led me to my grandmother's casket, and they encouraged me to kiss or hug her. Or maybe that's my imagination, but I recall kissing her, or wanting to because I had seen other people doing it. Although this was a lot for me to take in as a kid, I understood death, but I didn't understand the magnitude of how it would shape my perspective of life later on. The fear of abandonment was the first fear that I experienced. It crippled me and made me feel uncomfortable with the idea of death, but I was concerned that the people I loved the most would leave suddenly. It took me a while to process my grandmother's death, and it took years until my adulthood to fully understand the magnitude of how it affected me.

The other layer of fear I experienced was the fear of being harmed by others. There was constant verbal and physical fighting in the home that I grew up in. Although that was the norm for me, by nature, I was a loving kid who didn't like to yell or fight. I was always soft-spoken and kind to others. That is a part of me I have always prayed to God would never leave me. When you live in a violent environment, it can cause you to become violent as well. I believe God heard my prayer and answered me. There were plenty of times that I had a vision of becoming violent, but it was like God wouldn't allow me to act on it. Instead, He taught me to manage my emotions one situation at a time. He taught me the meaning of the scripture, Ephesians 4:26 (NIV), "In your anger do not sin: Do not let the sun go down while you are still angry," way before I knew it was His word!

While I lived in fear of others harming me, I feared harming others because of the intensity of the anger I could feel. As humans, we can feel the fire, meaning our bodies can feel hot, and our thoughts can get pretty dark and turn into demonic thoughts because of entertaining the anger. During my early adulthood, I would experience "blackouts." The medical term refers to a loss of consciousness, but I deem it to be a spiritual experience where I allowed the enemy access to my thoughts and behavior. Overall, I viewed this situation as giving my power and authority to the spirit of anger to take over for a limited time. Sometimes, all the spirit of anger needs is a few seconds or minutes, which can have significant consequences. Those consequences for me came with guilt and shame, which are still traits of fear.

Do you see a pattern here? The main issue is fear, though its layers cause many to focus only on anxiety symptoms, which isn't always correct. Fear can cause many traits, such as hatred. Fear also involves jealousy and envy. Throughout life, you may encounter traumatic events. Situations that can cause fear include a car accident, physical, emotional, or sexual assault, and witnessing first-hand or second-hand violence. Fear can also come upon you based on how a parent raises you. Growing up with one or both parents who used fear-based approaches to parenting can naturally lead you to rationalize decisions based on worst-case scenarios. Once these events occur, they can cause you to become immune to the emotions felt, negative thoughts, and behaviors around you. Ultimately, it causes internal damage you don't see until you decide you are ready to change your life.

Fear is an unpleasant emotion caused by the belief that someone or something is dangerous, likely to cause pain, or a threat. It can ignite anxiety, which is an intense and persistent worry and fear about everyday situations. There are different levels of fear and anxiety based on the person. While some people are high-functioning, a low-functioning person with anxiety may experience unbalanced behavior and thinking methods. It can fluctuate based on the triggers of the fear. Let's dive into the areas of life that fear can affect.

Mental & Emotional Wellness

In our natural mental and emotional state, we are supposed to feel peace and a sense of control, and to have a sound mind. When minimal stress is involved, the brain can be patient in identifying a solution or implementing a healthy coping skill to regulate the stress. If you have unhealthy coping skills when life experiences bring stress or an unfavorable, sudden change, you can have a short-term or long-term reaction to the experience. The difference between short-term and long-term fear is that short-term fear is more acute, meaning it will subside in a matter of minutes, hours, or a few days, whereas long-term fear will interfere with your daily life. Such as issues with sleep, an inability to control racing thoughts, even during pleasurable activities. Short-term fear can cause your mind to race about the fearful incident, temporarily shut down, or feel burnout, while long-term fear can cause you to feel high anxiety or panic, where you're not able to control it or stabilize it with coping skills. It's more beneficial to address long-term fear with a medical or mental health professional.

When someone does not adequately address symptoms such as stress and anxiety, they can lead to chronic stress and anxiety disorders. When emotions arise with stress and anxiety, they can create negative thought patterns, such as fear about different areas of your life. Fear can cause a physical response, such as numbness and shutting down, to avoid feeling the anxiety. There is typically one area of your life that you fear most. For example, if you experienced abandonment as a child, any ounce of stress can trigger fear of abandonment in adult relationships. Long-term fear can present itself as depression with feelings of hopelessness, loneliness, or overall dissatisfaction with life. Once anxiety or fear take root in the body, they can cause tension in the shoulders, back pain, or shortness of breath. Overall, every body system, including the digestive, nervous, cardiovascular, respiratory, brain function, and musculoskeletal systems, can be affected. Depending on the symptoms, your body can trigger issues with multiple systems.

Physical Wellness

Our physical bodies pick up what's going on in our minds and feel it. Our brains and bodies constantly communicate positive and negative thoughts and emotions, which are spread through neurotransmitters. When there's intense fear, our nervous system becomes unbalanced. As the nervous system connects to the heart, it can affect blood pressure and cause physical health problems, which weaken our immune system. If you've ever felt nervous or fear for an extended period, you have probably built up fear in your mind and body to a state where it affects your energy or pain levels. This can cause fatigue, sleep disturbances, or frequent headaches. Extended periods of time can go from hours to days without being able to stop the thoughts or emotions of fear and anxiety.

Behavioral Effects

When a person has fearful thoughts that are difficult to regulate, they eventually create behaviors. These behaviors can cause a person to create a new identity. A standard behavior that fear produces is avoidance. Fear can cause people to avoid situations, environments, or anything that triggers anxiety. Procrastination is another behavior many people exhibit, stemming from a fear of failure. Fear can cause a very creative person to become physically stuck and unable to take their ideas from their mind and put them on paper. While procrastination is a typical response to fear, it often creates more fear and anxiety in a person's life because the desire to succeed or complete a task can be just as intense as the fear. When a person isn't able to manage their negative emotions, they may have difficulty managing positive emotions.

When I was growing up, I often tried to be perfect, like working hard to do well in school and at work, and doing more than was required so people would notice. This behavior caused me to feel depression that led to me never being satisfied with the good I did; I always felt that I could do better. What I later learned was that fear was teaching me to stay stuck and to focus on my flaws rather than my strengths. The moment I started focusing on what I could do was the very moment I began avoiding negative thoughts and feelings of fear. It wasn't an overnight process, but it resulted from peeling back layers of fear that had become my identity since I was a child. The Bible speaks of plucking up roots that God didn't plant (Matthew 13:15). I applied that scripture to any fear I had and learned to trust the Word. I saw immediate results. That is when my faith grew and caused me to believe the word and repeat it. Over time, I gained more strength in the word and had less negative thoughts and fears.

Another common way that fear interferes with a person's life is through addictions and escapism. These are behaviors I know all too well. They can include substance misuse, overeating, or excessive entertainment to escape fear. If you battle any of these, keep reading. Today is the day that you will claim freedom from these challenges! God's desire for your life is to thrive in excellence; you cannot do that if you are fear-ridden.

Social & Relational Effects

If you've ever watched the news or scrolled through social media, you may have seen a common theme of arguments on podcasts or content where men and women are debating with each other. There are many reasons for this, but for the sake of this book, we will look at how fear plays a role. Fear can persist from childhood into adulthood through the relationships and social settings a person is in. It affects a person's mind, leading them to develop unhealthy perspectives about themselves and the world around them. Fear harms society because it prevents us from walking in the natural order of how relationships are supposed to flow. As humans, we are supposed to connect mentally and emotionally; however, fear has caused many individuals to keep themselves at a distance, erecting imaginary boundaries. This can lead to difficulty building healthy relationships and bonds within family dynamics and friendships. People who live in fear can have cognitive distortions so deep that they either don't allow themselves to get close to a person or have an intense fear of being alone, and they remain in unhealthy relationships. Those types of relationships can cause a person to experience low self-esteem and self-abandonment the longer they stay in them. The fear of loneliness is a silent killer of a person's self-esteem. It will tell a person, "Having someone present is better than being alone." That belief in itself can convince a person to accept verbal or physical abuse from a person because, in their eyes, the person meets the criteria of helping the person not to be alone.

Fear gets the best of individuals when it causes them to isolate themselves from the people who love them out of fear of rejection or embarrassment, leading them to believe others will judge them for their personalities. This type of belief can lead a person to have poor communication skills, causing them to withhold information about themselves or even avoid confronting issues. Failing to address fear internally will eventually lead to a lack of social interaction and unfulfilled needs.

Professional & Financial Effects

On a professional level, fear delays the development of skills and talents. It can cause a person to overlook gifts and keep them on a hamster wheel of spiraling, trying all kinds of hobbies that look successful based on what they see another person succeeding at. It's important to note that everyone has unique talents; individuals must look within themselves to discover their own. If not, it will lead to a setback in their careers and deny them opportunities. This fear typically comes as a thought such as, "I am not good enough." That statement alone can make you feel as if you are missing out on something a potential employer needs. When we look at the data on the world's most successful people, we see a pattern of high confidence and boldness. Faith is what a potential employer seeks; however, if you constantly talk yourself down and minimize your gifts, others will feel the same way about you. Why? Because people will eventually see what you know about yourself: the issues in your mind and heart. That's why many successful people lack skills. I believe that the combination of the two produces the most remarkable results.

Doing the opposite of what fear tells you to do would require you to stop rejecting yourself and start taking risks in career opportunities. It will also require you to make investments in your education or business, which will require not only finances but also time and attention. Today is the day that we eliminate all connections to imposter syndrome. The name in itself tells you it's a false title because you are a real person, with genuine talent and endless possibilities. It's time for you to ignite the fire inside of you, and stop putting the flame out!

Spiritual Effects

If you're reading this book and you have unmanaged fear, then it's more than likely you have a lack of faith. Yes, I said it; you don't trust God like you say you do. As believers, we must speak faith and feel faith. It can't just be on our tongues, but we must have it in our hearts. Fear leads one to question God's will, word, and abilities.

Sometimes, it causes people to question His entire existence; we see this in those who have left the faith and those who refuse to believe. When I think of the spiritual effect of fear and how it plays in human lives, I'm reminded of the children of Israel who murmured and complained on the way to the promised land. Many of those individuals did not make it because they leaned on their own understanding of who God was and allowed fear to interfere with their faith. Literally, fear ate away at some Israelites so much that they died. Did you know that fear causes you to live a dead life? Therefore, tackling fear is so vital. Experiencing God's word, will, and entire existence brings us life! So it's time to stand up, WARRIOR, and combat every component of fear that is dragging you down!

Scripture Meditation: 2 Timothy 1:7 (KJV) For God hath not given us the spirit of fear; but of power, and of love, and of a sound mind.

Biblical Affirmation: I take on the spirit of power, love, and a sound mind. I command all fear to leave my mind and my life!

BONUS-Practical Tools:

- Improve what you see with your own eyes. Your home environment should have things that represent the more significant parts of you. Here is a list of things to consider when shifting the decor in your home:

    - i.e., accolades, certificates, souvenirs from places you've visited, pictures of family and friends

    - Statues of animals

    - Colors you genuinely like!

    - Can you rearrange the look of your home every year? If you are wondering why, it's because the brain gets accustomed to everyday things and needs controllable changes to stay stimulated.

Knowing Your Authority in Christ

The relationship with Christ allows you to walk in your authority. But what should one do when he or she doesn't know their authority? This is simple. You commit to growing the relationship with God. By doing this, you will naturally build your spiritual health. While it sounds easy, it can be challenging because some unseen barriers may cause you to slack in building up your spirit. Growing up, I recall having a burning desire to learn more about God, so I would attempt to read my Bible. I was an avid reader, so I wanted to start at the beginning of the book, and I never considered starting any other way. I would read Genesis and find it difficult to understand and keep up with the structure of the word, so eventually, after 2-3 chapters, I would grow bored and sleepy. It felt like clockwork every time I tried to read the Bible.

Meanwhile, I could sit in bed for hours, reading a mystery novel. It was a concern for me because I couldn't read a full chapter and comprehend what I had read; however, I could read a 400-page mystery novel in a weekend. Eventually, I lost my love of reading mystery and adventure books in my late teens. My reading focus grew to urban novels that addressed adult matters, and eventually my desire to read the Bible dissipated. The topics ranged from sexually explicit material to content glorifying organized crime. I read about topics in the books I had no business reading or seeing at that age. I believe that made me uninterested in reading books for adventure and increased my curiosity about romantic relationships. Over the years, I've learned the power of knowing my authority, which I will categorize into three steps: surrender, knowing His will, and the posture of discipline.

#1: Surrender

To walk in your authority, you must know how to surrender to God's will for your life. As a babe in Christ, I recall trying to bargain with God by picking days, times, and specific events when I wanted to surrender to His will. I thought it was acceptable for me to engage in one sin because it was "normal" by society. Also, because of my relationship with sin, I had formed a belief that I was in control of it and that it wouldn't control me. Looking back, I can see how I allowed myself to be programmed to think that engaging in a "little" sin is okay as long as I'm not doing "too much." That was until I learned that following some of God's commandments was disobedient. I started off thinking there was a hierarchy of sins, with some producing more problems than others. But then I learned how willingly living a life of sin opens up the door to more sin and compromise. At some point, I had to look at the issues in my life and determine their root causes. I soon discovered that most of the problems stemmed from my desire to operate in free will. God gave us free will, so why give it if I can't use it? I then reflected on the outcomes of my life because of walking in my free will, and it wasn't a pretty sight. I concluded I did not know what I was doing, and the temporary pleasure from my decisions was causing long-term, ugly consequences. Through diligent prayer, fasting, and Bible reading, I received many revelations about the root cause of my life. It was deeper than operating in free will; it was about my rebellion towards God and His original design for humans. The stories and wisdom in the Bible helped me understand how my life would be better off operating in God's will.

#2: His Will

Knowing His will is another phase of understanding your authority in Christ. To understand it, read the scriptures to learn what He desires for His children. As you pray, study the Bible, and listen to God's voice, He will reveal specific plans for your life that are unique to your calling.

God's will is for everyone to be saved through faith in Jesus Christ, according to 1 Timothy 2:3-4. Jesus' crucifixion on the cross washed away our sins. Knowing our authority in Christ is the beautiful gift we receive from God, apart from our works. But of course, there are additional components to God's will that will enhance our lives.

We are called as believers to live holy lives (1 Thessalonians 4:3). It has many benefits, but the critical part is that we must decide to no longer engage in sin. Making this choice is what it means to have a repentant heart. The action of a person accepting Christ is no longer engaging in sin. We must not only state that we take Christ into our hearts but also align our actions with it. Truthfully, some sins were more challenging to let go of than others. This may also be your story, but there came a time when I had to choose between serving God or serving my flesh. The thought of disappointing God was more painful than letting go of the sin. I hadn't realized how much sin was crippling me until I read the Bible and grew in faith about what God's will meant for my life. You may have a hard time trusting His will, but when faced with a life-or-death situation, it will always be easy to choose God. I encourage you not to let things get to that point; surrender easily, and your life journey will be more effortless. So keep reading your Bible and allow the Holy Spirit to guide you to holiness without resistance!

Love God and others. Matthew 22:37-39 highlights God's request that we love him, others, and our neighbors with all our hearts. Do you know how challenging it is to love people who don't love us back? It is tough, but there is a guarantee that operating out of love will cast out hate from any situation. Our love for others allows us to spread God's love, and we know that the world could use more and more of it every day! The world is lacking in this area, so if we do our part, we don't have to worry about the world's wickedness overtaking the youth of the future. We are called to treat others as we would like to be treated. Every seed we plant, such as our words and actions, will produce its kind. Overall, God's will is that we love Him and love others with justice, mercy, and humility.

Throughout Scripture, there is a mandate to give thanks and rejoice (1 Thessalonians 5:16–18). When you observe patterns of behavior that reflect the fruit of the Spirit, take note and apply them to your own life. Scripture contains many accounts in which rejoicing and worship led to victory in battle. I equate this with spiritual warfare, which everyone encounters at some point. Every human can feel spiritual warfare through emotions or thoughts. Have you ever felt fearful, recalled a scripture such as "The joy of the Lord is my strength," and immediately felt calm? Reciting God's word and giving thanks is a strategy to defeat the forces of warfare. It confuses the emotions and negative thoughts because you stop focusing on the bad and feed your spirit with good. You have created a plan to cope with the emotion so that it no longer controls you. That's the beauty in your rejoicing and thanksgiving! God's will includes gratitude, prayer, and joy in all circumstances. Try your best to do this during the good, bad, ugly, and indifferent experiences in life.

God's will is also for us to do good works and share the Gospel with others, as highlighted in Ephesians 2:10. Doing good works extends to every area of our lives, including how we parent, how we show up as employees, and how we use our creative gifts through writing books and singing songs. Overall, every action we take should correlate with our good work.

An essential component of God's will is that we must trust in His plan! Trusting requires us not to believe what we want to think, but to believe what God wants us to think. Letting go of our understanding after living a life of trials and tribulations can cause us to resist trusting His plan. Still, as Scripture states, "God is not a man, that He should lie" (Numbers 23:19). There are many parents, pastors, leaders, and authority figures who have led astray many in their families and communities for many years. These individuals weren't living how God intended. We are all called to follow His will, and they have followed their own. Trusting in His plan will produce better outcomes for all His children. As Jeremiah 29:11 states, "For I know the plans I have for you," declares the Lord, "plans to prosper you and not to harm you, plans to give you hope and a future."

#3: The Posture of Discipline

The posture of discipline means striving to remain disciplined in believing that His will is best for you, no matter what your flesh desires. If this describes you, understand that God's love for you supersedes your own desires. His love keeps you safe when your flesh urges you to take risks.

Discipline is more than a word; it's an action. It takes a lot of mental strength to put the thought into action. I recall several attempts to discipline myself with what I ate and how I exercised. But now I understand that my desire stemmed from something shallow, even if I wanted to look and feel different. I grew up taller and larger than most of my peers in elementary and middle school. I was told by peers that I was an unattractive person, and because this is how my peers viewed me, I rooted myself in that identity. The one thing that made me feel unattractive was my weight. I recall the comments and snickering of others. During that age, I tried my best not to allow it to affect me because I had no desire to be friends with people who talked poorly about me. But later on in life, their words penetrated my soul and made me feel I wasn't good enough. So the only solution to that uncomfortable feeling was to lose weight. Over the years, I tried a myriad of diets and exercises, ranging from diet pills to Tae Bo. I would eat rice cakes and drink Slim-Fast shakes, but I never could maintain consistency for long. Overall, throughout my life, I would waver in my diet and exercise habits. If I didn't receive results, I would give up and return to eating poorly and not exercising. The one motivator that would consistently cause me to start the process would be the thought of how my peers viewed me and the possibility of being less attractive than others. This painful process eventually led me to explore my negative beliefs and look inward to see how my perspective on life needed to change. What I soon discovered was that I had a poverty mindset and that I would need to unlearn a lot of bad habits. Eventually, God showed me it was the relationship that I lacked with Him that caused me difficulty in maintaining discipline. Through the power of prayer and fasting, I learned that denying myself food in order to spend more time with God and gain greater control over my flesh led to an improved relationship with food. The authority that you have because of Christ is inevitable. It is time that you put on the full armor of God and step up in your authority.

Scripture Meditation: Joshua 1:9 (KJV) Have not I commanded thee? Be strong and of a good courage; be not afraid, neither be thou dismayed: for the LORD thy God is with thee whithersoever thou goest.

Biblical Affirmation: I have the power to tread on serpents and scorpions, and over all the power of the enemy: and nothing shall by any means hurt me. (Luke 10:19 KJV)

Understanding God's Promises

God's promises are versatile, and unique for every time period in our lives. His promises are truthful, transparent, and reliable. The promises that He's given us in the Bible for every life situation are timeless. The promises have no expiration date while we are living on this earth. Understanding them requires studying the Bible to gain revelation from the Holy Spirit regarding the promises for your specific life. John 3:16 informs us that believing in Jesus will grant us eternal life. Eternal represents a promise that is never-ending. This promise is so important that it will extend beyond our time here on Earth. The good news is that it will extend to the next generation of our bloodline. That's the power of understanding God's word. The stories of Abraham and Moses are great examples of how a covenant with God affects generations throughout the years. The magnitude of God's grace and mercy surpasses anything that fear has done or could do in your life. When you hold on to His promises, they consume negative thoughts and bring mental clarity with confidence. However, it is mandatory that you understand His promises for your life so that you can properly come into agreement with them.

Over the years, I've heard too many people reciting scripture while also complaining. If I had a dollar for every time I heard a person say, "I'm a child of God" or "God knows my heart" I would be rich. Listen, scripture tells us that God searches the heart for all things. It doesn't say that He searches the heart and accepts the things in the heart just because you are His child. There's a reward for righteousness, not for foolishness.

When you allow yourself to understand God's promises, it becomes easy to recognize them when they come to pass. God is not a genie. He's promised us certain things so that we can rest in them with reassurance and do His will. Your heart's desires are more than likely His desires for you, but you have to sever ties with fleshly lusts and desires connected to an identity other than Christ. Words of wisdom that can help to shift your entire existence are to seek God for yourself and remove any learned beliefs and habits that cause you to miss who God truly is. When you study the Bible and meditate on His word, you discover God has given us hundreds of promises. These promises range from the promise of marriage to the promise of healing. I'd like to reflect on a few that I feel are essential for readers of this book who are ready to defeat the spirit of fear.

Covenant with Him:

God has a fantastic way of speaking to us through the scriptures about how He makes covenants with His children. Many people can hear God's voice audibly through dreams, thoughts, signs, symbols, and visions. A covenant is simply an agreement or pledge. In Genesis 17, God appeared to Abraham and promised to make a covenant with him and to increase his offspring in number, making him a "father of many nations." When God desires to create a covenant with you, He will approach you in some form to make a covenant with you. God calls all His children to agree with His will for their lives so He can fulfill His plans on earth. There are things that, as humans, we will never understand. The depths of God are far beyond what's written in the Bible and what humans have experienced. But we know that His plans for our lives are good, and if we want what He wants for us, we agree that it's best for us. Most of the time, we do not understand, which is why we must walk in faith. When you can discern how God speaks to you directly, you feel an instant sense of peace with each promise He gives you. I've found that He speaks to me in a small whisper that can feel like a gentle command. But it comes from a place of authority. When He speaks in this way, I know that the instruction will benefit my life in some capacity. To gain understanding of what I hear, I pray and ask specific questions depending on what I hear. I sometimes wait in silence for the response, or I'll get clarity during a random moment of the day.

When I think of a covenant with God, I think of a relationship with Him. Relationships naturally occur when you are getting to know someone and experiencing life with them through an activity and/or environment. You would typically communicate with the person regularly about various topics and share your honest opinion, so they get to know you. The beautiful thing about God is that He already knows us; we are the ones who need to take time to explore learning who He is. A covenant with God is about honesty, accountability, faith, and obedience. Learning the simple facets of the relationship with Him will help you seek Him for guidance in everything you do. Why? Because He knows you best, and going to Him will solve all your problems. And remember, the relationship cannot be one-sided, meaning you only seek God when you feel like talking or need something. It's a two-way communication line. Build the relationship intending to listen more to gain understanding than to talk or pour out demands.

Marriage:

Since I was a little girl, I have desired marriage. I'm not sure if this is what most young girls' desire, but for me, it seemed like it was the best way to get through life. I grew up in a single-parent household; my parents were never married, and my mom was in a long-term relationship with my siblings' father. Throughout life, I promised to hold on to my virginity until marriage. I had this desire because my godmother instilled this value in me. She was the only one who would tell me to keep it, which is why I admired her throughout life. You see, I didn't grow up around people who were happily married; I saw people who were married but unhappy. Unhappy as in there was a lot of arguing, fighting, and infidelity. Viewing those relationships gave me an idea of what I didn't want in a marriage, and I thank God it never made me fear marriage. But I grew up not knowing what a healthy relationship was, so I accepted toxicity because in my mind, it wasn't nearly as bad as what I witnessed growing up.

However, one day in January 2020, I listened to a YouTube video where Tony Gaskins spoke on waiting for sex until marriage. It was at that moment that a light bulb went on in my mind. "Bingo, I must wait until marriage if I desire true love." Later, I realized God was planting a seed in my mind to guide me closer to Him. It wasn't about waiting for sex; it was about understanding the natural design for sex, which was for a husband and wife! I then went on a mission to understand God and who I was supposed to be and to seek Him to heal me so that I could become who He originally intended me to be. That journey led me to understand that my desire to marry stemmed from God's desire for me to marry. That was a comforting feeling that I didn't want to lose. So, I trusted that if I denied my fleshly sexual desire, then marriage would come. I soon learned that I would have to battle with my flesh because it didn't desire what my heart wanted. It took a few years to get it according to God's will, but I made it, and God honored that by giving me a husband—one whose heart represented Christ's. God doesn't just desire you to have marriage; He desires for you to have all of Him! And the best way to do that is to be intentional with seeking Him and understanding His promises to you.

Healing:

God is nothing short of fantastic when the topic of healing comes up. Throughout the scriptures, you see Jesus going from place to place healing women, men, and children because of their faith. If the children didn't know how to have faith and their parents did, there was healing. Simple as it is, walking in faith regarding healing is more challenging than usual. Why? I think it's because when we are in the middle of feeling low, fatigued, and battling with an illness, we tend to hyper-focus on the symptoms. Doing this can cause us to have low confidence, but it can also make us have faith in the illness itself. Learning God's word is the only way to combat coming into agreement with the disease.

Whatever you are feeling, speak the opposite about your life and body! Did you know that giving your body a command will cause it to heal itself naturally? It sounds simple, but it's not. As a human, I know this far too well; if I don't feel well, I will say I don't feel well and then focus on everything I think in the moment. This is an incorrect way of walking in faith. We must learn God's Word and apply it at the moment! For example, instead of saying that I'm not feeling well, speak Proverbs 3:8 over your life. God's word is more than enough to combat any illness. We must also be sensitive to the Holy Spirit, who gives us the strategy not only for walking in faith but also for taking steps to be obedient to what God is calling us to do to complete the healing. If I were to be 50 lbs overweight and had health complications because of the weight, I could believe in God for healing; however, I need to be practical with how God can do that. This is when prayer truly matters. I would pray for a divine strategy and strength to see God's plan through. Having faith in God will cause you to diet, exercise, and make adjustments as He leads you to. It's not about having faith with no action behind it. The actions we take are how we express our faith!

Sleep/Rest:

There is beauty in rest. Rest is essential. If you do not rest, you will experience the opposite of rest, which is burnout. Burnout in your home, work, relationships, and even within your passions. Why is rest necessary? God, our Creator, took His time to create everything in the universe, but did so in increments. He didn't operate like a robot that remained alert and moving 24 hours a day, 7 days a week. Since our bodies get tired, we need to rest to avoid burning out. Did you know that if you train yourself to work nonstop, at some point your organs shut down because of the stress you place on them? Our bodies can heal when we rest, but health problems can happen if we are always working too hard. Rest is more than sleeping and sitting still; it's also resting in God's word so that worries aren't running haywire through your mind. God has promised to give us rest if we cast our cares upon Him (1 Peter 5:7). Casting our cares means we need to take our worries or fears and hand them over to God.

We can do this through a simple prayer, such as, "Lord, you said in 1 Peter 5:7 that I should cast my cares upon you, so I am handing over the financial stressors that I have to you, walking in faith that you will provide me with the strategy to build wealth so that finances aren't a struggle for me. I will be a good steward of the tools that you provide me. Amen." You can cast your cares as often as needed, so your mind learns to walk in faith according to God's word. Repetition is key when understanding the word. It allows you to respond with faith, and it is a natural prescription for calming the nervous system. If you've never tried it, give it a chance!

Protection:

The troubles that you face cannot hold you bound unless you allow them to. For example, if you've been in a situation where you thought you had no choice but to choose between the lesser of two evils, then you are being deceived. Believers should not make choices that satisfy humans and contradict God's standards. When we look at the political, school, or healthcare systems, we may see traditions that leave us feeling hopeless. We must remind ourselves of who God is and what His Word says about how we should operate in these areas. One thing that we should do is pray for these individuals and systems to repent and do God's will. We should also pray that God has mercy on them. Not enough believers respond in this manner; instead, they allow fear to take over their hearts and minds, which causes them to spew hateful words about others and the systems. The power and authority that we have as Christians can either cause a nation to get worse or get better. When people have difficulty regulating their feelings about these things, discord grows among believers, causing more division than collectivism. This results in an infestation of the very things we, as believers, have the authority to bind spiritually according to Matthew 18:18. If we do not bind them, they grow spiritually and physically on earth. This behavior causes more problems than we can imagine! Scripture, like 2 Timothy 1:7, reminds us that God has not given us a spirit of fear but of power, love, and a sound mind. Meditating on these promises can strengthen our faith and give us the power that we need to navigate through life.

Scripture Meditation: Casting all your care upon him; for he careth for you. 1 Peter 5:7 KJV

Biblical Affirmation: I walk in faith and trust the Lord to help me navigate through all life circumstances.

Humble Prayer

Praying from a place of humility gives birth to a deeper sense of connection to God. It eliminates worry and sweeps away the need for control while allowing you to rest and surrender. The time is now to surrender to the endless possibilities of what God can do. In doing so, you will build your faith in what you are believing Him to do for you.

Philippians 4:6-7 encourages us to bring our concerns to God in prayer because seeking His peace can help us remove fear. The power of prayer is reliant on your posture. Is your posture of prayer only to seek Him when you want something, when you're down and sad? Or do you pray without ceasing? Studying the Bible has shown me that many people who come to God with an open heart hear Him and see Him move in their lives. Many people go to God in prayer when they are in a broken place. The scripture calls for us to come to Him when we are brokenhearted, but what about seeking Him for other things? Prayer should be a lifestyle you practice in every facet of your life. It's beneficial to pray when you are happy, sad, content, confused, or angry. There are no emotions or thoughts that God can't handle. He is present to help us sort everything out, not just some things. There's great power when you include Him in your everyday life. We should also remember that He has given us a Comforter, the Holy Spirit. This means that while we navigate daily tasks and stressors, we have a guide to lean on.

Throughout your journey, you may have prayed a brief prayer of thanks to God for a meal you were about to enjoy, for being saved from a painful experience, for a job promotion, or even for being blessed with a car. These prayers are minimal when you reflect on all that God has done for you. These types of prayers do not take away from how we acknowledge God. It's highlighting that, as children of God, we can do more. People often minimize the word of God and the things the Bible requires, presenting them as optional. There are requirements for walking in righteousness, which provide us with God's protection against the enemy of this world.

We spend much of our time stressing and complaining over things that are not in our control, and what does it give us? It brings more frustration and anxiety. Now, in the world, do we really need more of that? No, we need to feel the peace of God and know the posture of faith to maintain so we don't waver from it. All it takes for most people is to be triggered by one thought, another person's opinion, a flashback, or something wrong to happen, and suddenly, they feel frazzled. How long does it take for you to regulate your emotions and shift back into the feeling you had before being triggered? It depends on the severity of the situation and can range from minutes to days, and for some people, even weeks!

1 Thessalonians 5:17 states that we should "Pray without ceasing." Our brains have thousands and thousands of thoughts a day. Thoughts can be harmful, positive, and neutral. Some are rational,

while others are irrational. Because of the increase in mental health disorders throughout the past 10 years, I'd assume that people are thinking more about the negative than the positive. Is it possible that we are mismanaging the tool of prayer that God has given us? Stewarding the things that God has given us is an essential skill that we should all try to master. It is showing God that you appreciate what He's done for you and that you haven't forgotten His love, grace and mercy. Stewarding what he's given us is an act of faith. One example of mismanaging prayer includes focusing on things outside your control rather than praying humbly for peace or a strategy to work through them.

Throughout the past few years, I've discovered that prayer must be intentional. In various ways, God answered some of the simplest prayers I've prayed. The answers came through my hearing His voice through my thoughts, receiving a prophetic word, or having a dream or a supernatural encounter. Sometimes I would open up a social media app, and the answer would be right there. I learned that asking God for things versus asking for strategy and wisdom yielded greater results. Why? Because when I tell God I want to change for the better, I need a mindset to receive all that I'm asking of Him, and of course, it must be in alignment with His will. Asking God for things is us wanting God to do a thing for us versus asking God to show you how to do something. Both are necessary prayers to use; however, one will require you to take action, not just walk in faith alone.

Many times throughout my life, I have felt paralyzed with worries about finances while pushing myself further into debt. The patterns that caused me to have worries were never my focus until I asked God for wealth and riches. Now, that may sound familiar to you if you have asked for more money, thinking it will resolve all your money issues. I had attempted to do it my way for years, but I had to be fed up with myself before I sought God for proper guidance. My flesh would always say that I wasn't making enough until God revealed to me I was making more and more money every year, but mismanaging it. I had to go back and look at past salaries to get a visual of the numbers and where the money was going. What I found shocked me. I was purchasing whatever I wanted when I liked it, because I had the means. But I had reached a certain age and realized I had saved no money for retirement. The pain of that reality hit me hard, and my money problems went from worries and fear to pure guilt and sadness. The sadness came from the reality of who I was and from the fact that I hadn't taken care of the blessings God had given me. I was abusing them for a moment of pleasure, instant gratification, which left me with dissatisfaction in the long run. The agony drew me closer to God, where I longed to understand how to steward the money. I realized I did well at making money, but I sucked at keeping it. This situation was like my hair-growth journey. I could grow hair, but it would lead to a pattern of breakage, which I had difficulty overcoming to meet my hair goals. It's interesting how one area of my life showed up in other areas. See, that's the power of fear and how it causes you to live a poverty lifestyle mentally, emotionally, and physically. With my hair, I was afraid of wearing it, so I adorned it with wigs that kept me in a state of hiding. The same way I tackled the fear of money is the same way I'm tackling it with my hair–addressing it head-on in faith and with divine strategy. At some point, we all need to grow spiritually to combat all areas of lack in our lives. Therefore, the power of prayer is essential. It causes you to seek God with your whole heart, to hear His voice and His instructions, so that He can renew you from the inside out.

If you're reading this book and have yet to seek God with your all, I encourage you to take a chance at surrendering everything you thought you knew so that He can mold you into who He created you to be. Now go ahead, pause this book, and give him your best, honest, and raw prayer.

Here are some simple prayers that you can use as a starting point for building your prayer life:

Salvation Prayer:

Father, thank you for your love, mercy, and grace. I come to you to confess my sins and ask for forgiveness. I believe Jesus died on the cross for my sins, and I accept Him as my Lord and Savior. He is the way to salvation. I ask that the Holy Spirit fill my mind, my heart, my body, and my spirit to guide me in all aspects of my life. Father, I thank you for saving me. I am committing to living a life that honors you. Teach me your ways. I trust in Christ through faith to renew my mind. Amen.

Faith Prayer:

Father, I thank you for searching my heart and keeping me on a path of righteousness. I thank you for protecting me from dangers, seen and unseen. I thank you for your love, grace, and mercy. You've seen me during my good times and bad times, but Lord, you've never left me nor forsaken me. By faith, I walk in assurance knowing that you are with me, leading me into all truth. By faith, I lean in on your desires for my life. At this moment, I am choosing to trust you and let go of all my fears. Lord, let your will be done. I pray in the name of Jesus. Amen.

Family Prayer:

Father, I come to you with humble praise. I thank you for delivering my family and me from the hands of the enemy. We haven't been perfect people, and I repent on behalf of the family bloodline for the decisions we've made. Lord, I pray you search my heart and forgive us for our sins. Every covenant that doesn't align with you, I come out of agreement with. I speak Psalm 91:11 over our lives, for you have commanded your angels concerning us to guard us in all our ways. I pray that everyone in my family will accept salvation and follow your ways. Your ways are what's best for us, so teach us and guide us, leading us into all truth. I thank you for saving my family. In your name, amen.

National Prayer:

Father, I thank you for creating the heavens and the earth. This world has many things that I feel a great deal of disappointment about, but if I come to you, you can provide me with clarity and comfort. I don't understand everything that's going on, but I know you are the Creator of this earth. I am repenting on behalf of the nation for turning its back on you and not following your ways. Lord, I pray you cover us on this earth and have mercy on us. You are the God who brought us out of Egypt and saved us from captivity. You are a God who doesn't lie and never fails. I'm praying that you hear my cry and save us from the wickedness of this world. By faith, I trust you will fulfill your perfect will here on earth. In your name, I pray. Amen.

Scripture Meditation: And the peace of God, which transcends all understanding, will guard your hearts and your minds in Christ Jesus. Philippians 4:7 NIV

Biblical Affirmation: I will include God in my daily life. Prayer is easy for me.

Meditate on Scripture

Meditate on the word day and night, and night and day. All humans meditate on something daily. Meditation is simply focusing on one thing. That one thing can cause you to create ideas about it that result in your spending a significant amount of time on the topic. Ideally, it's healthy to focus on one thought, sound or thing that can bring a sense of peace and clarity. However, the mind can do the opposite as well, which can bring mental stress and discord.

God instructs believers to meditate on the scriptures throughout the Holy Bible. My understanding is that it helps to pull us in closer to God's voice and provides us with simple instructions for living, such as navigating through life challenges and knowledge that will be effective in our decision making. Meditating on the Word can help a believer make sound choices. Imagine not knowing God's desire for our lives and making a decision that has long-term negative consequences. When I look back at my early adulthood, I wish I had known how to make better choices. Sometimes the flesh can get the best of us, and we make decisions that can go against God's word. When we know His Word, it's easier for us to decide from a place of wisdom.

There's great power in including the word of God in your daily meditation. Whenever we sit and repeat a thought or experience in our minds, we are meditating. In Greek, the word meditation can refer to caring for something, careful attention, practicing, or devising. When I think of the word meditation, I think of the words strategy, intention, and agreement. We have these massive minds that are powerful enough to create ideas and experiences that are real and some that seem impossible. But in meditation, it shows that the mind can create a feeling, a thought, and a vision of a thing. The human mind has thousands of thoughts a day. When I think about the number of thoughts I have in a day; I notice they range from reflections on the past and present to hopes and desires for the future. My brain also thinks about information I've gathered from the beginning of my life until now, which is a lot of years of data collected.

The brain reminds me of a sponge; whatever we put in it, it will absorb. Some information may slip to the back of the mind, while some information stays at the front. Some thoughts don't occur to me until I have a triggering emotion or revelation that forces me to recall a memory. These memories can range from pleasant experiences to awful ones. Anytime the trigger occurs, I'm left with two choices: do I want to keep the thought or get rid of it? This is the power of meditating on scripture: it provides you with the wisdom to dissect your thoughts or reject them. Rejecting it involves being dismissive, minimizing it, coming out of agreement with the belief of the thought or avoiding it. Some thoughts will feel as if they are haunting you, while other thoughts feel easy to manage. I've learned over the years that God has given us the ability to discern whether thoughts come from Him or the enemy. And guess what? Sometimes it's neither; it's you who are creating the thoughts in your subconscious mind.

The subconscious mind is more complex than I previously thought. It stores information and can create patterns and habits that can have you questioning yourself, like, "Why would I do that!" or "Why did I think that!" My clear response to this repetition is to assess the issues of the patterns and identify what changes need to take place. That's how powerful the mind is; if you feed it something, whether that's knowledge, reflections, or a fear, over time, it will provide a full-blown consequence. Every thought that you have will give birth to an action. As you know, outcomes can be positive or negative. Therefore, what we choose to meditate on is essential. You must know what you're taking a risk for with what thoughts you allow yourself to reflect on. Thoughts come from anything that you experience, which we naturally gather data from through hearing, feeling, tasting, touching, and seeing. All five senses being stimulated can activate your brain to store information. We naturally do this without trying.

I learned the power of this once I started spending five minutes each night listening to an audio version of the NKJV Bible while reading along in a physical book. In early 2021, I was exhausted and burned out from practicing witchcraft, so I slowed down on it day by day. After nearly 2 years of studying and practicing New Age, the desire to engage with tarot reading videos and divination felt pointless, and my craving for deeper spiritual meaning grew. I had an interest in the practice because I was searching for an understanding of my life and why I had the challenges and gifts that I had. I was looking for God in all the wrong places and ended up losing myself as I drew further away from Him. After an encounter with God in bed, I cold turkey stopped engaging in the practices. These actions came from thoughts about my childhood and early adulthood. Building a relationship with God was something I attempted but fell short on. I didn't have any real-life examples of what it was like to have a healthy relationship, so it was easy for me to give up on praying and reading the Bible when I didn't receive an answered prayer. I now understand why, which was because of a lack of spiritual guidance from any authority figure in my life. But we all know that we can only use that excuse for so long until we take control of changing our lives, despite what our parents failed to do. I went through phases of trusting God but not understanding what actions I needed to take, so I would start and stop because, honestly, it was hard to trust Him, and I had no clue what it meant to trust a person. Everyone in my life had disappointed me, leaving me feeling rejected and abandoned. The moment I encountered God in 2021, I was desperate, and my ears were wide open to receive Him. I was heartbroken and needed God to mend it, because I knew I would make a poor decision and deepen the wound if I handled it! At that point in my life, I was tired of being afraid of bad things potentially happening and made a choice to allow God into my life so that bad things wouldn't happen to me. You see how my mind shifted when I walked in faith and not fear? Although the change came from a lot of repeated patterns and cycles of dysfunction, it arrived at the perfect time.

During my adolescent years, I tried several times to read the Bible. I would read a few chapters in Genesis, and I would fall asleep mid-sentence, never recalling a word that was read. My mind would drift off into thinking about the latest boy band or song I liked. I learned how to escape my reality at a young age, which caused me to dissociate from much of life and kept me in a state of mental fear. Although I kept the Bible in plain sight, next to my bed, I started a cycle of forgetting to pick the Bible up and never finishing the chapter previously started. So much time would go by before I'd pick the Bible back up, I had forgotten what I read, so I'd re-read the same scriptures until I took a hiatus from reading the Bible. I didn't completely turn from the Word; I carried an orange Bible with scriptures I could pull up during difficult times. The thing is, I only used it when I felt fear and high levels of stress. I don't recall picking up the Bible when I was feeling gratitude or when life was going good. When I look back, I wish I had had the knowledge I have now about the power of gratitude and the importance of expressing it to God. However, I was in survival mode, and I lived in that space mentally, emotionally, and spiritually until I had an encounter with God.

The encounter I had with God in 2021 is something I will never forget. It changed me for the better. God gave me a strategy to discipline myself in His word: listening to the audio version while following along with it in a physical book. I am a book reader, and only the Bible was hard for me; no other books were challenging! God strategically planted that idea in my mind, and it led me to set small goals for myself: to read/listen to scripture for 5-10 minutes. I kept it short at the beginning because I would get sleepy around the 15-minute mark. I really wanted to recall the scriptures I was reading so I could better understand them. One of my prayers before and after reading was that God would help me understand the word. I have always been a lover of knowledge, and this time I only wanted God's wisdom. I craved to know Him better and to understand my purpose on earth. At some point, I took my highlighter and highlighted words in the Bible that stood out to me. I could read a book and completely forget everything, but I learned in college that I had a gift for skimming books and would do well at absorbing some information, but not all. I started applying this skill while reading the Bible as well. Every thought during the time I spent reading the Bible centered on understanding God. I no longer focused on things that were outside of it, such as the latest song or life worry because when you want something, you'll discipline yourself to get it. This was my way of building discipline and of not allowing my mind to wander.

At some point, God revealed to me the importance of learning about the characters of the Bible, and He showed me how to focus on their characteristics and mannerisms. With this Bible study tool, I started studying the book of Joshua. I recognized the importance of being courageous. I believe God led me to the book of Joshua because I had lived a life of having a false identity rooted in fear, fear of how people would view me, fear of telling the truth, fear of people abandoning or rejecting me; it was debilitating fear. God showed me how to use the scriptures to build affirmations I would soon learn to love speaking over my life. Joshua 1:9 is where God instructs Joshua to "Be strong and courageous. Do not be afraid or discouraged, for the Lord your God will be with you wherever you go." This scripture became music to my ears, and I felt God was speaking to me directly. As I took that word God gave me, I wrote it in journals and on index cards and placed the cards wherever I could so I could see them. I even set alerts on my phone so the scripture pops up at various times of the day. I knew at this point that there was power in repetition. I believed that if I saw it enough and said it aloud enough, I would eventually memorize it and believe it. I also knew that memorizing it would help me apply it in every area of my life.

The true power of God is when we walk in faith; His word becomes a lifestyle that we live. For me, it first started with believing the word, applying the word, and allowing the word to renew my mind. The word is living, so the scriptures that we meditate on never die! Do you understand the magnitude of that good news?! It never dies, so it will always live on the inside of you. That's the privilege of meditating on His word; you not only read it, recite it, and become it, but your identity in Christ shines brightly through you. And that's a goal that we all should strive to have— having the mind of Christ, according to 1 Corinthians 2:16.

Overall, reading and meditating on the verses can rescue you from fear, which teaches you how to speak to the spirit of fear, and it ignites a power within that causes you to be more courageous in the faith, God's word, and who He created you to be.

Scripture Meditation: Peace I leave with you, my peace I give unto you: not as the world giveth, give I unto you. Let not your heart be troubled, neither let it be afraid. John 14:27 KJV

Biblical Affirmation: I will prioritize my day with scripture. I will meditate on the scripture day and night.

An Act of Faith

Imagine living in a world where you learned the importance of choosing God intentionally. I mean, trusting Him to the highest level possible during the most frightening situations. This is the importance of walking in faith; it helps us combat fear. Hebrews 11:1 defines faith as the assurance of things hoped for, helping us focus on God's power rather than our fears. I know what the power of keeping my eyes focused on God can do during a storm. While it wasn't easy to do the first few times, I found it was much more pleasant to do than sit around worrying about the matter at hand. I have a few stories to share with you about how God clearly spoke to me and showed me His power, and how my walking in faith would birth a great testimony.

Trusting in God was no simple walk in the park, but a few years ago, I had a legal matter to attend to in court. While I'm not ready to share this story yet, it's a testament to what God can do when you seek Him and obey His instructions. Back in 2023, I received a letter in the mail telling me I would need to attend a court hearing. While reading the letter, I felt so defeated that my body shook, and anxiety rose. I went from having a good day to having a terrible one. Instantly, thoughts of guilt over the decision drove me to feel sad. While on the brink of depression, I just wanted to lie down in my bed and go to sleep. The emotional pain was all too much. I started thinking back to how, if I had just said "No" to a matter a year prior, I wouldn't be in the situation I was in. You see, I had a complex about saying no; I thought it was a bad thing and felt obligated to say yes. But what was I saying yes to? It turned out that I was saying yes to things that would later on hinder me and drag the peace that I felt in life away. And it never failed; every yes led to me having to say no to something that I truly needed in life, which was a break, a nap, or simply a reset to life. Life had been hitting me upside the head since childhood, and I just couldn't understand why.

After reading the court's letter, I prayed and read the Bible rather than going to sleep, as the fear was telling me to do. Fear was telling me to avoid and escape, not to seek God. I recalled the decision I had made and questioned why the outcome had been so challenging. I remember feeling God's presence and Him telling me to keep my eyes focused on Him and that He would see that I got out of this situation. In that moment, I realized I needed to be better at going to God before any final decision. Anytime I leaned on my understanding, I would make an emotional decision. And honestly, nothing good ever came of making an emotional decision. This time, I understood better what God was saying. I then prayed some more, and I heard God clearly say, "You do not need a lawyer." When I heard that, I felt quite confused, since I had a piece of paper in my hand that stated otherwise. I then started asking Him about it, and although He told me I didn't need one, I scheduled a phone consultation with a lawyer. I thought that there was no way that He'd instruct me not to get one. After the call with the lawyer, I felt more defeated than I had when I read the letter. Why? Not only did I have a legal matter to deal with, but I also had financial stress because I didn't know where the money for legal counsel would come from. I started telling myself it would be okay to use a credit card, even though I was already in significant credit card debt and needed a break. After the call with the lawyer, I said an earnest prayer to God, asking Him to defend me as I was innocent of the matter. During that prayer, I also repented of my past and present disbelief and disobedience to God.

Following the prayer, God revealed to me that the instructions He had given me were all part of His promise to free me from the bigger issues I had been dealing with. I questioned that because how am I in a legal matter after being obedient? Then God talked to me about the steps it takes and the posture I must uphold throughout the process. He told me to walk in truth, patience, and love. I still needed more clarity on this because I was at my wits' end with the sleepless nights and guilt that I felt. But God was patient with me and showed me I wasn't in error and that the court wouldn't accuse me of doing something I wasn't guilty of, because He would defend me. He told me that sharing my truth was the only action that I needed to take, along with being confident. I felt that listening to Him had to be my only way out, because a lawyer couldn't give me the peace that I needed, especially if it was to come with more debt. I took the time to pray and fast, to continue seeking clarity, and to build my faith to walk in what God called me to do, which was ideally, nothing. That was a hard task, but I needed to see what life would be like without panicking and walking in my emotions while making emotional decisions.

I felt a sense of peace on the day of the court appearance, but I was cautious about the conversations. In my mind, I thought I'd need to have a speech laid out to defend myself. I met with a member of the legal team's staff, and after that conversation, I let out a sigh of relief. The person outlined their goal for the court hearing, saying they understood my decision and would request my release from the matter at the hearing. It was in that moment that I knew God was the greatest lawyer, defender, protector, provider, and all the above! When I met this person for the first time, they somehow understood the case well enough to know I shouldn't be held liable for the accusations. I felt calm and silently prayed, thanking God that He had been speaking for me.

I sat in a room for a while before we entered the courtroom. When the judge appeared, I began focusing on being myself and showing up with courage and honesty. I didn't have to speak much, but when I did, there was a calmness in the room. I guess in my head I had imagined the judge being mean to me and minimizing my truth, but the opposite happened. I showed up and gave a small testimony, and I had faith that God would redeem me for the sleepless nights, guilt, and depression that I had battled with until the day of the court hearing. At the end of it all, I only had to sign off on a piece of paper, and the problem that I once had went away, because it was never an assignment that God called me to.

This period of my life lasted only a few weeks, but it felt like a lifetime. It would've been worse had I not listened to God's voice. However, I see it as it could've been better had I not panicked the way I did. But I know this was a lesson I needed to get through so I could understand God's power and the power of not allowing fear to drive my decisions. I had a lifetime of letting fear into my mind and telling me how to live my life, how to think, how to speak, how to act, just how to live which was never good because fear kept me in a paralyzed state of mind. It taught me never to give up on it because it was the driving force in my life. In that moment, I knew those emotions were telling me a false story, a story that didn't align with the visions I had dreamed of for my future. Fear was setting me up for failure, for never mastering my emotions, and it was teaching me how to allow my emotions to drive my daily thoughts and actions.

The court experience showed me that God hears our prayers, and if we silence our minds long enough, He will respond with a strategy. God gave me the plan to be patient and not take unnecessary steps. He showed me what true love was. In the court situation, God showed His love through His concern for my life, even in the small matters. When I wanted to call the lawyer for a consultation, He didn't discourage me from getting the information. What God did was highlight certain things the lawyer said out of routine. A routine that I didn't need because it would cause stress in the financial area of my life. God gave me a strategy to help me get on the right path to paying down my debt and not adding more. The relationship I had with money is another book in itself, but you see how fear almost led me down another rabbit hole that would've taken additional time for me to get out of? Fear provides a domino effect; it affects one area of your life after another. I've grown to learn over the years that if fear could do that, how much more could faith do?! It would do a lot more good as it would enhance the quality of our lives. And I mean, after these years of allowing fear to run my life, I had to give faith a chance. I had to allow God to renew and restore me to my original design and the path He intended for me. This led me to choose Him more and made it easy to part ways with fear.

Another incident where God spoke to me and saved me from having a terrible outcome was back in 2024. I had connected with an older woman, and she chose me to be a panel speaker for her women's conference. During the event's planning phases, I noticed disagreements, disorganization, and a lack of clarity regarding the event schedule. At first, I was told I'd get several incentives for participating, like lodging and transportation. I appreciated the incentives because I wanted to take part, but my financial limitations created a problem. These are things I informed the organizer of when I accepted the panelist role. The woman was loving and inviting in the beginning, then I noticed a shift in her behavior towards me. Instead of making an accusation about her behavior, I turned to God and prayed that He'd reveal to me what was going on. To my surprise, He revealed to me it wasn't a partnership that was within His will for me. First, I wasn't in alignment with Him, and I hadn't sought Him before deciding to be part of the event. Second, I had been idolizing the woman because she was older and I had unhealed mother wounds. I was in total shock at this discovery, but it all made sense. I didn't know this woman but was seeking a motherly bond. Her initial warm embrace caused me to want to have a relationship with her. Without truly knowing her, I had a high reverence for her. After prayer and repentance, I did what God instructed me to do, which was to remove myself from the panel. This hurt deeply because I wanted to speak at a live, in-person event and share my testimony of how God delivered me. But what hurt more is that I had failed to consult with God, and I could've been in a worse situation had I moved forward with participating in the event.

After apologizing to the woman, she immediately turned cold towards me and blocked me on social media. Then, an hour later, she texted me to let me know she wouldn't be able to remove me from the flyer. I didn't mention that she was advertising a flyer without me on it before I sought God and when I inquired about it, she said it was a mistake. So, her telling me this after I removed myself felt strange. I accepted her behavior towards me and moved on, knowing that God would connect me with the right people. Knowing that I could have avoided this situation made me upset with myself, but I had to learn the lesson. A few days later, I connected with a few ladies, and the following year I hosted my first in-person event. All along, God knew what I needed and what could hinder the plans that He had for me.

I am encouraging you to seek God first and walk in faith with the steps that He has ordered for you. You never know what He's protecting you from and what good things He wants to do through you.

Scripture Meditation: I can do all things through Christ which strengtheneth me. Philippians 4:13 KJV

Biblical Affirmation: I will walk in faith, trusting that God will see me through all of my troubles and victories.

Support from Your Community

Engaging with a community of believers provides encouragement and accountability. Hebrews 10:24-25 highlights the importance of gathering together. While scripture emphasizes the importance of fellowship, fear can cause you to avoid seeking support from people you do not know. But guess what?! If you did not grow up in a loving and healthy family that can guide you in love, then you may seek people outside of your bloodline for support. The Holy Bible speaks to the importance of servanthood, clear throughout the Old and New Testaments. Being a servant means you have a gift given by God, and that people will benefit from it. If you are bold enough to seek these people with direction from the Holy Spirit, you will find a friend, a mentor, or even a spouse along the way!

The Bible states it wasn't "good" for man to be alone, but also imagine a world where people didn't interact with one another, and everyone kept to themselves? Well, it can be tempting to think it would be better than how the world is operating now, but people who have healthy communities and support systems are more grounded and thriving. People with healthy relationships and strong support systems may be unknown to you because they focus on their own happiness rather than broadcasting it to the world. Have you ever noticed that more people are spreading negative thoughts and emotions on social media than healthy stories? While they are doing this, a flock of people either comes judging and condemning them or bonds with them because they can relate to the topics they speak on. This happens for various reasons. People thrive on convenience in relationships, and it can cause someone to avoid meeting people in person because "It's more work." I'd say this happens because people fear being rejected by new people, and it's easier to build relationships through trauma bonding. Although this is the case for some people, the trauma bond doesn't keep the relationship intact; it causes it to become a burden for one or more people in the relationship. This will cause the relationship to end in some form or fashion.

Not only are people building relationships through trauma bonding, I've noticed that some people maintain relationships with others because they don't want to start over. Suppose you have a person in your life who speaks in judgment toward you with put-down statements, but because you have no one else who will be present in your life, you decide to maintain a relationship, although it's toxic. You may think, "As long as I'm able to connect with someone, it's better than being alone and having no one." My response to that would be it's better to live in a world with people who treat you right than those who treat you wrong. If you want to be treated right by others, you must first create a habit of treating yourself right and not allowing people to hurt you repeatedly. Overall, this world is better lived when you have people who will listen, support, and provide sound advice.

While building a support system from the community, you must consider your needs. Are you willing to step outside your comfort zone and get help from a professional, or do you feel it's best to talk to a friend or family member? The people who love you the most can sometimes experience fatigue from offering emotional support or, sometimes, constant trauma bonding. Trauma bonding occurs when you and someone else talk about each other's traumas together in a way that brings you closer. This type of relationship can be unhealthy if there isn't a balance between the topics that you both speak on, and if only one person dumps their thoughts on another. These are the relationships that you want to avoid when seeking support from your community, rather that's through a professional or not.

During my healing journey, there was a period of isolation where I had to let go of every friendship I had. In some relationships, I directly told the person I was disconnecting from them, while others naturally ended because I didn't contact them. I also blocked some people because I didn't feel strong enough not to respond if they reached out to me. I sat and evaluated the relationships that I had and determined if there were signs of trauma bonding. I found that I trauma bonded with every person and had an anxious attachment style that was rooted in fear of abandonment and rejection. I realized I kept people in my life as long as they weren't blatantly disrespectful towards me. They could have subtle gaslighting references, but it wasn't enough to let go of the friendship. During this journey, I sought God for understanding of where I went wrong in every relationship. The revelations were mind-boggling but allowed me to accept the end of the relationship and no longer sit in grief.

I encourage everyone to take inventory of their relationships to identify what changes need to be made, especially if they don't have a healthy community. If you have relationships you'd like to maintain, it may be time to set an intention to reduce trauma conversations and focus more on bonding through your likes and interests! If you find that it's hard to set a boundary with that person, it may be time to consult with a mental health professional.

Being seen by a mental health professional can open up more windows of opportunity for healing and personal development. Although there's stigma in the mental health community, being a healer is a gift that God has given many professionals. If you look at any career, you will find people in it for the wrong reasons, but there are plenty who are there because they are called by God into it. Those who are called have a special way of evaluating, active listening, and understanding your needs. These are abilities that a close loved one or best friend may not have because of their emotional attachment to you or not having the skills to offer transformative feedback. This is where a mental health therapist would be the perfect fit for you.

My story is simple: I became what I needed, which was a therapist. Along my educational journey, I learned I had unresolved trauma. Before school, I didn't have a label for what I endured; I just knew that it was not normal, and I needed to understand how deeply it affected me. But I didn't attend school for myself; I attended it because I had a strong desire to help other people. It was innate, and I couldn't shake it. I tried several fields of work, all of which allowed me to serve! If someone had a problem, I wanted to help them find a solution. I had a special interest in the healthcare field and wanted to be a Nurse but after working at a hospital, as a Medical Records Clerk then a Certified Nursing Assistant, I eventually grew to understand that I loved listening to people talk through their problems and had a gift for being able to share a new perspective while offering tips to help them overcome the problem. This came as a shock to me while I was working in the nursing field. After feeling disappointed about not being able to enroll in nursing school because I had to work a full-time job, I started researching programs at a local university. As I read through the different programs, I locked eyes with the Social Work program. This was the moment that my world changed, and I decided that the calling over my life was 100% tied to a career in social work. Eventually, it led me to where God called me to be, a Mental Health Therapist serving the people as God instructed me to. And it's something that I absolutely love to do!

If you're reading this book and have apprehension about working with a therapist, consider the gift that God has given many and keep an open mind. You never know what God has planted inside of someone who is on assignment to help you. Yes, you! God never intended for any of us to do life alone; His children are in all professions all over the world. I encourage you to pray that He connects you with helpers who will support you on your healing journey.

There are other ways to build relationships within your community, such as connecting with members of the church you attend. Are you the type of person who prefers to hear the praise/worship, then the sermon, and then leave immediately after the church service is over? I used to be that person, but I eventually learned that if I stepped outside my comfort zone and socialized, I'd learn something new about myself and about others. While the individuals in the church may not be the emotional support you need, it can help you build healthy communication skills that could help you break free from social fears or poor social skills. If staying after church feels too overwhelming, consider attending the church's small-group meetings or a local group that aligns with your hobbies/interests. If you enjoy knitting, join a knitting group in your area. This is a great way to build community by putting yourself in different environments to establish healthy relationships that could lead to friendship!

Fellowshipping with others can help you grow your mindset by learning from those who have wisdom in areas where you may lack it. It can also lead you to help another person overcome their struggles or simply to talk about life's victories. It's powerful when you can walk with other believers and talk about the goodness of God rather than the defeats of Satan. Many people who struggle with social anxiety have overwhelming thoughts about how others perceive them, which prevents them from giving people a chance to experience them so that they have an honest opinion. Yes, we live in a society where people will judge you by your appearance, but guess what? There are just as many or more people who will judge you by your heart and the fruit that you produce in life. It's time to give people a chance to get to know you, while you get to know them, and break free from what your past relationships have taught you about life. The best way to overcome fear is to face it head-on and challenge its reality by doing the very thing it tells you not to do!

The time is now to step outside your comfort zone and overcome the fear that has been holding you back from experiencing life as God intended. There's so much power in building community; don't miss out on a person or group who's waiting to support you, love you, and experience you!

Scripture Meditation: For my yoke is easy, and my burden is light. Matthew 11:30 KJV

Biblical Affirmation: I can put all of my faith and trust in the Lord. He will guide me to all the right people!

Worship and Praise

Worshipping God can shift our focus from our fears to His greatness. It's an act of faith that causes you to feel the love and every word of God. While worshipping, you put down every burden and feel God's warm embrace. Imagine trying to reach God by phone to express gratitude, update Him on how your day is going, or just to seek His guidance in a matter. Also, in the background of your home, the TV is on, playing your favorite show. Suddenly, you get the idea to finish cleaning your home, so you get up from your seat. As you move, your mind starts racing, thinking about all the other tasks you still need to complete. These things would automatically cause you to be distracted and unable to approach God in a way that you are giving Him your full attention. If you've ever been on the phone with a friend or family member who would have side conversations with others while on the phone with you, remember how that felt. It may have felt like the person wasn't listening or interested in you. It could have also made you feel you weren't important to them and that they didn't value your time. See, this is how God may feel when a believer is calling onto Him but has so much on their plate that they cannot focus and give Him their undivided attention.

When you are calling on God, do it while surrendering. Surrendering requires you to let go of anything that could interfere with your relationship with God. While the Bible doesn't use the word surrender in the KJV version, it uses the word submit. One of the Greek definitions of submit is to obey. In the matter of worship, I'll reference Psalm 100:4: "Enter into his gates with thanksgiving, and into his courts with praise: be thankful unto him, and bless his name." This word sums up how a believer should present themselves to God through simple instruction. Worship shouldn't be optional in a believer's life; it is a requirement. Psalm 56:3 encourages us to trust in God when we are afraid. I encourage you to worship God in every emotion, season, and experience. Praise is a timeless act of faith. It teaches us it's natural to be vulnerable and guides us to vocalize our love to our Heavenly Father. It's a sweet melody when God sees our hearts and posture of worship.

Growing up, I loved singing songs. I would sit up in my room, play my favorite R&B music, and sing as loud as I could. Other times, I would sit in silence, make up songs from the top of my head, and feel at peace. Later in life, I learned through reading the Bible that God naturally made us to worship, but I was unaware of its significant power. Gospel music attracted me during times of distress, but I did not know it did more than just help me through the sad times. Have you ever listened to a gospel song, and the words resonated with how you felt? It would take you into a blissful space of peace, joy, and freedom. This is freedom that you may have only felt when we are sitting in the presence of God. This type of peace helps us to silence our minds and open our hearts. We live in a world where it's necessary to guard our hearts, but when sitting in the presence of God, our hearts are safe. It's safe for us to give Him our all and our best praise.

Worship and praise are so powerful that the combination of them causes the enemy to fail. Which results in your walking in alignment with the plans that were created for you. There were many times when I cried out to God in song, and He responded immediately, bringing peace and calm to my mind, body, and spirit. The biggest weapon that I learned to use wasn't a prayer or recited scripture; most times, it was my tears. Honest tears and believing that God was the only one who could help me with the challenge I was facing. This led me to being intentional with the relationship that I was building with God. I didn't want to only approach Him during the sad times; I wanted to experience Him while I was going through the good and confusing moments. I became intrigued with leaning into His promises and hearing Him respond.

While His responses don't always feel good, I knew that His feedback and instructions to me were for my good. Many times I'd pray while feeling anguish, disappointment and sadness. Not only did He dry up my tears, but He defeated the giant of fear and anxiety that was attacking me. Each time this happened, it was during the night hours, and He would give me rest to where I'd wake up the next morning feeling no negative emotions, only feeling safe. Each time I did that, I learned that worshipping God needed to be intentional. If I believed He was a comforter, I would approach Him for that, which led me to letting go of vices that were unhealthy for me. Repetition is valuable. It's important to repeat the steps and routines that bring you closer to God, not those that draw you away from Him.

In 2 Chronicles 20 of the Bible, there is a story of how worshipping God brought deliverance to a nation. I learned that when we go to God directly with our concerns about an enemy attack, He will respond on our behalf by fighting the battle for us, requiring us only to praise Him. But I understand that there must be a level of courage and boldness in our praise and worship. This doesn't mean that it has to be loud; it's all in your heart posture. Sometimes I praise Him with my arms wide up and times when I've lain still, no movement but giving Him my best. His presence can be intense to the point where I only want to lie down and not move, focusing on Him. Keeping your eyes on God causes mountains to move, and this is where the impossible becomes possible. Whatever worries you have, they suddenly fade.

Sitting in God's presence during worship and praise shifts the atmosphere, turning a prolonged problem into a permanent solution. Praise and worship are simple, but it's hard to sit still. To master this, you must teach yourself how to sit still–meaning, you redirect every thought of worry back to a word that God has given you, a scripture, or what you are having faith for. When you learn to discipline yourself, you will witness the power of God and His power come upon you. It's a sweet feeling. You'll never leave it once you experience it.

Worship and praise allow us to enter the gates of heaven. Often, it has helped me feel as if I were having a face-to-face conversation with God himself. I've experienced chills running up and down my arms, my upper body swaying side to side, and all heavy emotions being nonexistent. When I worship, I want God to know that He is the best, my one and only, and praising Him is essential to me. I've learned that, to do this, my motive for praising and worshipping must be righteous and holy. I should not approach Him with what He will do for me, but be thankful for what He has already done.

Allow God to be the center of your attention, show Him you are full of faith and ready to be led. Build a connection with Him that fear, shame, lust, greed, or anything else will not separate you from that connection. Prioritize Him and watch Him shift the dynamics of your life. He will lead you on straight paths that no man can steer you away from. He will deliver you from destruction and wickedness.

During times of famine, you will feel an overflow. You will understand the depths of how Abraham felt when God called him a friend. Being a friend of God means that you have sought Him, laid down your life and have access to Him to discover His mysteries.

Prayer and worship do not have to be separate. In fact, both allow us to act out our faith. Romans 12:1 highlights the importance of how we present ourselves to God and how our lives can symbolize "proper worship." In the KJV text, it's described as "reasonable service," which is a service rendered or to perform a sacred service. We should meet God in a state of praise and worship, without strings attached and with a servant's heart. I can imagine that having adoration for the one who created us is like a sweet aroma to the Father, as described in 2 Corinthians. Worship and praise cause us to walk in faith, which draws us near to Him.

Romans 12 also reminds us that the way we live is worship. We should live a life that's pleasing to Him. A life that follows His standards for our way of living is our worship! But what is that supposed to look like?! For one, we should keep our minds and bodies pure, which is why we must learn the ways of God so we aren't constantly fighting different battles with fear. Living for God is not always easy, but once you have learned to trust Him in every season of your life, it helps dissolve worry more quickly than not living for Him. Learn to let go of the thoughts, habits and vices that He says are not pleasing to Him and stop making excuses for you to keep doing the very thing that disappoints Him. It's difficult to let go of those things because you fear what life will be like without doing what you're used to. Or fear of who you will be without it. This is an identity crisis, and you won't walk in your full authority, that's given to you by God, if you allow fear to guide you. If you've lived in fear, you'll know that it's harder to live a life with fear than with God. If you believe that it's the other way around, it's because the enemy has told you a lie. It's also easier to believe a lie when you see evidence of the lie that's being told. Your worship is what you believe; you can worship God or the devil. Either way, choose which to believe and which you prefer.

Let me help you take the guesswork out. If you believe in God, then you'll be able to walk into the promises He has in store for you, which are outlined in the Bible. If you knowingly or unknowingly choose the devil, which are the lies you've come into agreement with, you'll walk into the promises that the devil has designed for you. Both have significant consequences; one is clearer than the other. And while God's promises offer a life of peace, the devil provides a false representation of it. John 10:10, one of my favorite scriptures, gives a great example of the two, which states that, "The thief cometh not, but for to steal, and to kill, and to destroy: I am come that they might have life, and that they might have it more abundantly."

Fear diminishes your quality of life, leaving you empty-handed and lacking in several areas, while faith brings you a life that gives you more. More joy. More peace. More freedom. More love. An overflow of God, which we could never have too much of. If I haven't convinced you enough, just know that the terms and conditions of choosing to do life in faith with God bring clarity in all areas of life, while the enemy will cause chaos and confusion. Choose the one that will give you something that He cannot go back on His word about! God's promises are sure, never lacking in substance and evidence.

Scripture Meditation: He that dwelleth in the secret place of the Most High shall abide under the shadow of the Almighty. Psalm 91:1 KJV

Biblical Affirmation: I will honor my mind, body and spirit how God has designed me to. I will be a good steward of my life and praise God, always!

Healing from the Root of Fear

Did you know that there is life after fear? Meaning that you can live a healthy and productive life without fear. It's all about understanding how to cut the roots of fear out of your life. To do that, you must know precisely what created the fear that you struggle with. Knowing the significant life events that caused the fear will help you plan a strategy to let go of it. Earlier in the book, we discussed how fear affects a person's life, but we didn't dive deeper into how fear is born in a person's life or the revelation that God gave me about how it came into my life. Personally, fear came in through various avenues, some of which you may relate to, others you may not. Overall, dive deeper into why fear showed up in your life and what it was assigned to distract you from.

I grew up in a single-parent household with my mom, siblings, and my mother's partner, who was also my three brothers' father. From an early age, I learned to fear people and conflict. See, I wasn't in a typical household where there were subtle disagreements among adults. From a young age, I witnessed verbal and physical altercations that would often keep me up at night. I recall a time when we had a family event at our home, with the adults drinking, listening to loud music, and having a good time. As kids, my siblings and cousins would be in the house during that time, having fun playing together. They allowed us in the same rooms as the adults, so we heard and saw everything. The family events at our home were usual, and our family got together frequently. But during a social gathering with family and friends at our house, I recall being in the hallway during my mother and her partner arguing. I also recall there being my mom's close friend and maybe a sibling in the same area of the house. I don't recall what was being said; I just remember everyone yelling and using vulgar language. At some point, I saw a person hand my mother a knife, and within the flash of an eye, I saw blood seeping from her partner. Everything happened so quickly that someone moved me out of the way, and I only recall an ambulance coming to the home and taking him away. While I recall little other than that, I know that my nervous system hasn't been stable since that incident. It's a memory that has frequently flashed through my mind over the years, especially in adulthood. While it became normal to hear and see them argue and fight, it triggered something inside of me that wanted me to run and hide with each verbal and physical altercation following that one, but I couldn't. I had nowhere to go, so I would stand and watch, saying nothing but feeling heavy emotions.

Over the years, the arguing got worse because, at some point, they started arguing at midnight, and I often jolted awake. When that would happen, it would be hard for me to stop listening to the yelling. I eventually started turning on my radio to drown out the noise. Because I didn't know how to express my feelings and often wondered,

"What difference would it make?" I turned to music and reading for comfort. Music and books were fun hobbies at first that turned into coping mechanisms for me. The relationship I built with both activities over time made me dependent on them to calm me down whenever I felt anxious or stressed. So from that day on, when I saw my mother stab her partner, I felt unsafe living in our home. My mind constantly feared that my mom, siblings, or I would be harmed, and I felt helpless since I was only a child and couldn't do anything. So I did what typical kids do: I became accustomed to the arguing and fighting while trying to focus on what was within my control. I learned from these experiences that witnessing violent acts, like fighting, arguing, or seeing someone hurt, can make you fearful. All of which I encountered in my household, but also witnessed in other family environments outside my home.

The root of fear grows within us based on what we allow into our eye and ear gates. The Bible speaks to the importance of protecting these parts of our bodies, but most of us do not understand the full extent of why. I'll keep it simple: anything we absorb can influence us and/or alter our identity. Typically, these thoughts, behaviors, or feelings can sneak in during childhood and become normalized. Then, when we realize they aren't reasonable beliefs or traits to have, it's hard to part ways with them. This is how it was for me, specifically growing up watching scary movies and celebrating Halloween. As a child, I enjoyed the fall because I was born in October, and it is a beautiful time of year. I started taking part in the holiday as a child because it's naturally a tradition at school and in my family. Around that time of year, there are a lot of cartoons, movies, and music that go along with the theme of Halloween, which is to be afraid! But being afraid of ghosts, goblins, witches, and gory things led me to having nightmares and negative visions in life from a young age. What seemed so pure and innocent later opened my eyes to its unnaturalness.

If you're reading this and celebrate Halloween, you will probably think I am overthinking this. But tell me: are you battling a fear that's hard for you to shake? Did you grow up like me, watching scary movies and celebrating Halloween? If so, I encourage you to dive deeper and recognize that, although things may appear normal, they can be abnormal, especially when they affect a natural part of our brains and bodies. If you've watched a scary movie, then you know that the intention of the movie is to keep you in suspense, never knowing precisely what is going to happen next. This instantly puts your brain on alert and your nervous system in a state of distress. Some may think that this is normal, but I'd like to challenge that belief. Consider how a child experiences this when introduced at a young age, especially since a child's nervous and brain systems are not fully developed. This intereferes with the development of the brain, because it's not God's natural design for us to experience such things. Introducing these types of activities that disrupt the thinking process and nervous system would alter it from its original state. There are some things we are in control of, and others that are outside our control. Taking part in activities that we are intentional about should be well-calculated. But we live in a society where whatever is popular and fun in the moment is acceptable. Therefore, taking part in these activities at a young age led me to delve deeper into their spiritual connections as I aged. Everything that we listen to, watch or absorb leads us through a door. Either a door that God has for us or Satan.

Later in life, I grew a liking for scary movies and became an avid horror movie watcher. The only horror movies I couldn't watch much of were the ones with a lot of paranormal activity, and that only happened after years of watching them. Most nights after watching these movies, I would have a hard time sleeping. My brain would focus on the components of the movie and create new scenarios, which would turn into my feeling symptoms of paranoia. One way to ease those fearful thoughts and feelings was to remind myself that the movie wasn't real. However, that only lasted so long because I would sometimes watch documentaries about killings, shootings, and other brutal actions. No matter how scared of these shows I felt, I couldn't shake the desire to watch them for the entertainment. When I look back at these experiences, I think it was strange that these types of movies intrigued me, but I felt obligated to watch them. But it wasn't always scary; it was entertaining and artistic. The character's acting and the details in the movie amazed me. For me, it was art. For my spirit, it meant that I was being controlled and my state of mind and body were being altered. That's my truth, and the truth of many individuals, if they take the time to examine the root causes of their issues rather than just look at the surface. Despite this being part of my identity as a child and adult, God delivered me from it, and I no longer have a desire to watch horror films.

As I started writing this chapter, the Holy Spirit highlighted several other experiences in my life that formed the root of my fear. For the sake of time, I will spare you the details and focus on the main points. While this is my story, I encourage you to pray and ask God to highlight the experiences you've had in life that have been the root of your fear.

When I look at my parents' parenting style and how they are as individuals, I notice that they have fear-based beliefs, which naturally shows me they parented me through fear. Their parenting style included fearful words spoken and fearful actions. With my mother, the fear came generationally, handed down to me through DNA. Not only does DNA cause us to have the same medical risks, it passes down personalities, physical traits, and talents through the family bloodline. For my father, I experienced abandonment from him physically and emotionally since my adolescent years. Because of that, I'm going to assess that my father's abandonment was rooted in fear. My guess is that it could've been fear of being a father, fear of being rejected, or fear that he wasn't good enough of a person. Whatever it was, it caused much pain throughout my life, and I'm sure it did that to other people connected to him. He inherited the behavior, so I don't blame him because his father abandoned him. See how having the same DNA as a parent affects you? That's what the root of fear does! It causes your perception of yourself and others to worsen, so each experience that you have causes you to grow further and further away from God and His original design for your life. It starts small and grows like the common cold or flu. If you don't have the skills to contain it and get rid of it, you end up suffering with it for life. That's my drive for writing this book: to stop the effects of fear and improve the quality of individuals' lives. I have an optimistic view that the world will be better when we are in one accord about the small things that cause the most significant issues. Meaning, once we walk in alignment with the kingdom of God, life will be less of a struggle.

A few other root causes of fear are beyond our control, but once we understand them, we can control our perception and behavior towards them. Trauma is a major cause of fear because when you experience something as significant as it, you can't turn off the reality of it occurring. It can grow to be a thorn in your side if it's not properly addressed in the beginning. Trauma can have a massive impact on your perception of life, especially if the incident is causing flashbacks and painful episodes of reliving the moment years post the experience. Imagine what this does to your nervous system and how it can create a lifestyle of being in fight-or-flight mode. That's not a healthy way to live, but it's the truth of how trauma affects a person. The other way fear can grow within us is through our insecurities. There's no doubt that in life there will be things we like and dislike about ourselves and life. Most of the time, we can put more emphasis on the things that we dislike about ourselves, which causes higher levels of stress and anxiety. This leads to fearful thoughts about who we are, and it can take a toll on how we navigate through life. Imagine yourself putting more focus on the qualities of yourself that you like and enjoy, rather than feeling weighed down by the things you don't like. Focusing on what you like will give you more strength, insight, and motivation to work on what you don't like. This will free up time, emotions, and energy spent on useless and negative self-talk. Overall, the relationship you build within yourself will dictate how you experience life outside yourself. Now is the time to tackle fear and stop letting it take over your life. It's time to sever ties with it and live freely.

Scripture Meditation: 1 John 4:18 (KJV) There is no fear in love; but perfect love casteth out fear: because fear hath torment. He that feareth is not made perfect in love.

Biblical Affirmation: I am letting go of anything that causes me harm! I cast down every thought and behavior that is related to fear. I will walk in faith and accept my healing.

The Power of Walking in Faith

I didn't understand God's strength because most of my life I had been walking in my strength. In my mind, the strength seemed great and mighty. The strength that was brought about through resilience from childhood trauma endured. The strength that you have to muster up to protect yourself. An unspeakable strength, because where else would it come from if I couldn't trust the adults around me? I thank God for bringing me to a place of understanding His strength versus the defense mechanisms that I had because of trauma, and how the strength that He gave me would supersede my highest expectations.

Walking in faith isn't an option; it's mandatory to walk in peace, love, and freedom. It's the foundation of what God requires from us; without it, fear easily manipulates us. Imagine living in a world where you are courageous and never have to question your beliefs. As a believer, it would allow you to walk in the image of Christ and to complete the tasks that God assigns you. It would mean that you wouldn't have worries about who God is and His Word. You'd be able to stop fearful thoughts from formulating into a full sentence or scenario. You'd know without a doubt that it was a fear. Your discernment would be 100% on point, and you'd be able to know God's voice versus Satan. The beauty in all of this is that you can get there, no matter how much fear has crippled you throughout the years. It may have affected you in the past, but this is where you take control. Did you know that you have 100% power and authority over fear? Let me remind you of Luke 10:19, where Jesus says, "I have given you authority to trample on snakes and scorpions and to overcome all the power of the enemy; nothing will harm you." This word provides you with total assurance and access to defeating fear. All you have to do is know the word and apply it to every situation that involves fear. If you memorize this word, your spirit will be whole enough to respond to fear without you experiencing the effects of fear, such as a racing mind, unstable nervous system, and all the other symptoms your body feels when you encounter fear.

Walking in faith ignites a fire inside of you to follow through with tasks that you're assigned to. It allows you to minister to God's children when He tells you to. Through rough seasons, it will keep you faithful. It provides you with a pure heart. It gives you a warning when you are close to a danger zone. That danger zone can include manipulation, defeat, procrastination, burnout, and hate. Faith needs you to be all in, or else it'll struggle to show up when it matters most, but it'll be easy for you to have faith in the small things. You may not understand the magnitude of faith, but you must learn faith as if you were a student learning a new skill. It takes time, patience, and perseverance to walk in faith. But God is so faithful that it will be easy to surrender to it because faith provides you access to our Father.

According to Matthew 6:33, God will add all things to us if we seek Him and His righteousness. Do you understand what that entails? It means that you will receive everything that you need and more. You will collect the things that God has in store for you, one by one. This is where faith is necessary: you may not get everything at once, but when you walk in faith, you have a level of patience that helps you embrace every day, journey, and season God has you in.

Faith is confidence in what we hope for and assurance about what we do not see (Hebrews 11:1). But the beauty in it all is that when you are in proximity to God, He will tell you what He has in store for you. Be willing to shut out the noise in your mind and remove any limiting beliefs that could interfere with your receiving His promises. God is unmatched and has the most unconventional ways of showing up in our lives, which will most times feel like a mystery. But it's really no mystery when you walk in faith and consistently seek Him. Overall, you'll just need to take the time to get to know Him, because knowing Him is a requirement to walking in faith.

Throughout this book, there has been guidance on navigating feelings of fear and on ways to tackle them so they stop affecting your life. Rejecting fear shouldn't be hard to overcome, yet many people deal with it daily. If we look at the mental health statistics of the world, we see they are rising every year. I have a few ideas about why this could be, but I'll keep them to myself for now. What I know is that when we walk with the world, we will have a worldly outcome. When we walk in the kingdom of heaven, which is godly things, we experience life differently, not just in a spiritual sense but in a physical sense. You perceive life differently and respond to matters differently. But we are all human and have real emotions. Sometimes those emotions can be so big that they overwhelm our ability to handle them. Mastering your emotions shouldn't be your primary focus in life, where it nags away at everything that you do, from how you sleep to how you show up in relationships. There's so much more to life than living in fear, and it's up to you to decide how you will do it.

I want you to be inspired by the life lessons I've learned, realizing that you're not alone and never will be. When you seek God, you are turning to the only One who can help you with every single question about the problems that you have. He's the ultimate solution. The way. The truth. And the light! So, whatever dark thoughts and feelings you are having, hand them over to him. The power to walk in faith will help keep you strong in believing that God can do all things. It will help you avoid trying to walk in your own strength. It teaches you to surrender to the things you don't know. The things that you desire to have access to, but God has shielded you from. How amazing is that? A God who will only give you what He knows you can handle and not more than that. That's a promise to hold on to!

I want you to remember that this book is a guide, and you should pray about everything so that God can lead you to the perfect strategy for your situation. To wrap up this book, I want to reflect on the chapters you've read thus far and offer some gentle reminders.

1. Learning how fear affects you helps you manage it better. If you learn the ins and outs, you will gain control over it.

2. Understanding your authority in Christ is essential to knowing who you are.

3. God has given us many promises in the Bible. If you don't know what they are, then how will you know why He's called you to do certain things?

4. Prayer allows you to build a relationship with God, not to receive things from God.

5. Meditating on the scripture day and night doesn't have to be hard; all it takes is effort, and the Holy Spirit will do the rest!

6. Acting on faith brings significant results. It will have a lasting effect on your life.

7. People were meant to walk this earth with others. Don't be afraid to find your tribe!

8. Praise and worship beautifully combine adoration and reverence given to God. Give God your best praise as often as you can.

9. The root of fear can run deep, but it's not too deep that God can't reach it. He can uproot anything that He didn't plant!

Now, go on and be great. You serve a mighty God who will give you the strength to conquer it all!

About the Author

Shawnee Neal has over a decade of experience as a mental health clinician. Shawnee has helped individuals of all ages overcome challenges such as depression, anxiety, trauma, and life stressors.

Driven by her own childhood experiences and a deep passion for mental health advocacy, Shawnee has become a trusted voice in her community. Beyond her professional work, she is a devoted mother and philanthropist who volunteers her time to uplift local youth and older adults.

As a speaker and event host, Shawnee shares empowering messages rooted in biblical principles, inspiring others to find hope and purpose. Her life's mission is to serve as a vessel for God, spreading the Gospel of Christ and positively affecting the lives of those she encounters.

Connect with Shawnee!
Email: shawnee@alpinesempowermentagency.com
Website: https://alpinesempowermentagency.com
YouTube: https://www.youtube.com/@ShawneeP
TikTok: https://www.tiktok.com/_shawneep

<u>*Check out Shawnee's other books on Amazon:*</u>
- *Shifting Your Mindset: A Guide to Overcome Depression, Anxiety & Trauma*

- *Free From Captivity: A Memoir of a Generational Curse Breaker*

- *90 Days to Writing & Self-Publishing Your Book*

- *Walking in the Fruits of the Spirit: A Guide for Single Women on Their Healing Journey*

If you want to book consulting services, email Shawnee with your inquiry!

www.ingramcontent.com/pod-product-compliance
Lightning Source LLC
Chambersburg PA
CBHW062148100526
44589CB00014B/1744